Love the Universe in You

Love the Universe in You

Dean Pusell

iUniverse LLC
Bloomington

LOVE THE UNIVERSE IN YOU

iUniverse books may be ordered through booksellers or by contacting:

iUniverse LLC
1663 Liberty Drive
Bloomington, IN 47403
www.iuniverse.com
1-800-Authors (1-800-288-4677)

ISBN: 978-1-4697-3575-7 (Softcover)
ISBN: 978-1-4697-3576-4 (e-Book)
ISBN: 978-1-4759-1399-6 (Audio)

Printed in the United States of America.

iUniverse rev. date: 09/20/2013

Introduction

My first open-eyed, conscious peek at the mystical beauty as an absorbing infant was the cool, quenching, vast freedom of a fresh and crisp blue sky. This little heart's rhythm of openness was never vulnerability; it became pure awe instantly. This baby step started the growing journey of intrigue and appreciation for our life's abundant treasures.

Two weeks after my sixteenth birthday, I broke my neck after hitting a submerged rock while diving into the ocean. My two best friends saved my life.

A new awakening confined to a wheelchair, to never walk again, brought me a totally enigmatic depth of understanding of human reality. My world had now slowed down, from what I liked to what I loved. Words, colours, music, nature—all had a distinctively acute, powerful, and unique interpretation.

This book is an accumulation of scribbles from the heart and is projected through mind to hand; the truth of myself writing this book was to heal others by being a being of honesty. I hope you enjoy my little piece of our world.

Smiles of peace,

Dean Pusell, 2012

Contents

Our Fire and Moon

I hear your soft roar,
Crackling and spitting sparks,
Hissing to breathe the crisp breeze.
Your warmth is like a lover's aura.
From blown, ripped ribbons of yellow light
To brittle, broken orange puzzles throbbing,
The dusk rolled out old stars.
As one fell, all the shiny rain robbed melting.

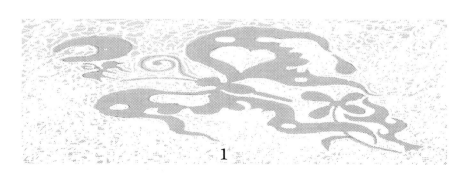

The Diamond Web

Do you see the breath
In the dance of the leaves?
Raindrops on the golden spider web
Shine like a mesh of soul weavers.
Do good with your essence;
You can trust again,
Mend that thread,
To live in the beauty of presence.

Sipping Gravity

All great love and energy,
I welcome your freedom.
Most sacred vibe,
I smile at your essence.
The peaceful spirit of wilderness
Encompasses your messages clear;
Our home is so connected,
But we're woven temporarily here.

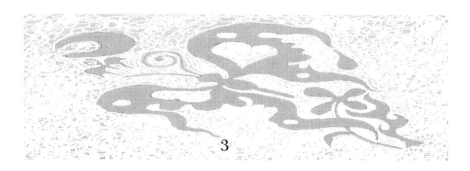

Her Celestial Drift

Dusk's lone star fell,
Hit the soul of a princess.
She fell into me,
I fell in love.
So brightly Venus walks this world
In smile and truth.
She's my bliss
That sacredly soothes.

The Soul behind Words

It's all true:
Dream, wake, devour—
A concept of you,
Ingesting another hour.
Pure empathy strengthened that heart;
It surfaced a thought.
We try one day of no war
And look within to what humanity's taught.

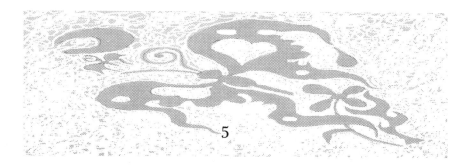

In Hail

As you sink you fade our dusk;
The fireball journeys on,
Sharing its soft warmth.
Winter is closing to stars.
Scattered glitter slowly illuminates
Like smashed diamonds on earth's oil,
Blinking in the black blindness.
My princess comes to me to coil.

I Still Mind

We all drink from the sky
And bleed to the ground;
What was permanent
Is all unbound.
So I re-twine my heart
Till it beats warm;
I flow a peace
To heal the torn.

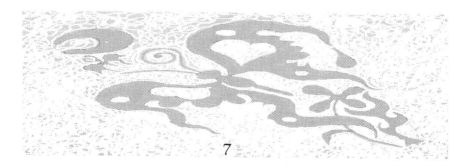

Being Nourishment

What's gained in ego, measured
When courage and patience prevails?
Fear and craving melts
When unrecognisable to hail.
Naked disappointment controlled you, prisoner;
You made the lock, you can make the key.
It will only mean much more
If you set yourself free.

An Imperfect Harmony Sifts a Buoyant Love

You knitted a dream,
That of a tangled web;
It was retied with smiles
As you grew away from fear.
Blessed in earthy colours
And creature trust,
I'd dwell listening to my mind's echoes,
Deciphering what's love and lust.

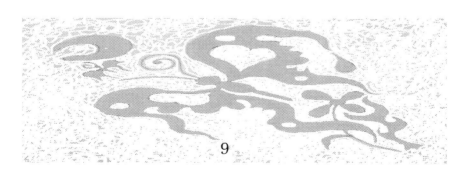

The Shimmering Sacredness of Us

Circling a scream, she glides through the sky;
Safer to cry quiet sometimes.
So refreshing, these droplets;
The prey emptied its head.
Look up again,
From eagle to angel.
She meant no harm—
She was just listening to your heart.

<u>The Sanctuary in You</u>

Breathing dawn's songs that echo,
This winter sun rises from dreams.
I've found a new love,
Absorbing you inside of me.
Amongst the tallest silhouettes,
My heart vibes small to a hum;
Breathlessly I'm alive in this garden,
Free as one, belonging to one.

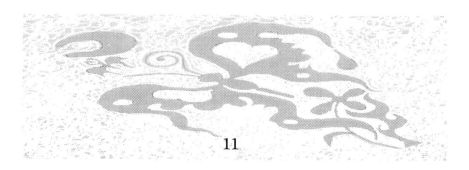

A Vibe Came Smile

He denies his master,
Lost in an ego cloud.
You are still leashed to mortality,
So maybe expire proud?
Too much self is madness,
Insatiably empty.
Don't let the mind deafen the heart,
Nor hoard your love in the temporary.

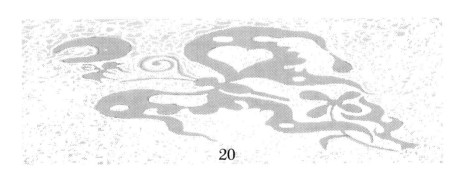

Her Lantern's Flame of Trust Breathes

Scratching slowly from heart,
Here's pulse to paper.
My angel's weary eyes
Dim to the earth.
I promised your light,
I'll blow the clouds to stars
And give you the seed of truth,
Nurturing sacredly the growth of me and you.

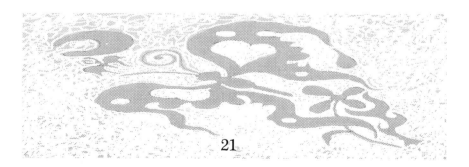

21

Miss

I rode the day's fire out,
Chasing for her beauty.
This spirit surfaced to stars,
Reconnecting with escaping time.
Alone I'm a ghost,
Until mirrored eyes raise me real',
There I'll nestle home,
In the friend that feels.

The Velvet Blue Tear

Unforgiving wisps of winter
Twist and revive my shadow;
Responsibility is taken,
Awaiting her love that was given.
Acoustic thoughts bounce,
Searching the sun-bleached sorrow.
My love's pretty eyes of earth
Believe in us, a world of tomorrow.

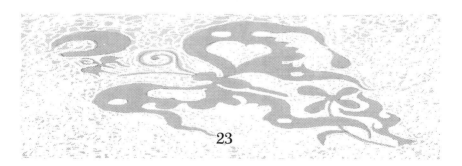

<u>See Now</u>

You want to come, star sail?
As souls, no feathers,
Love higher than the Babylonian zoo,
And see within, outside.
Below bellows the found lost puzzle,
Pieces of peace torn,
Let's makes smiles, not bullets,
To grow love, not wallets.

<u>Love You</u>

The pure silence floats the stillness,
Though birds and insects squeal to dream.
Dusk just smashed slowly
And sprayed some stars.
A spark to a blaze chases breath,
Awakening the shadows
All teaching me,
Us.

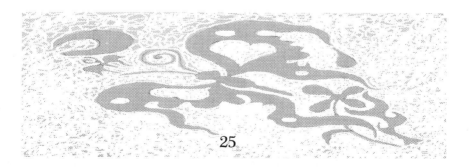

Interconnected Treasures

I trust this trail glistening
Is of the one angelic honey,
No wings but earthbound smiling,
Absorbing the sweetest gifts.
Violet flowers float the tranquillity;
As a butterfly ripples ringlets of diamonds,
The pond's stillness returns,
Within learning body, mind, and soul bonds.

A Tangent Slant of Humility

Even with closed eyes,
I can feel your warmth,
Hear your heart,
And taste your sweet essence.
To me you're beyond this physical realm,
Past dreams and wishes.
You're a lantern of bliss,
Floating me in mortal kisses.

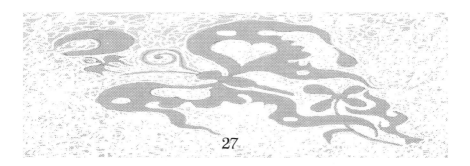

The Spirit Promised

Sway shadows around me,
But don't climb in.
Reflections shimmer the third eye,
But it's now that I begin.
Drift, little dreamer,
Sail that light my way.
I will be one with your flame
Till the last breath of our day.

A Tingle Reminds

The softest ringlets reflect her eyes;
A smile twirls my heart,
And slowly that spark grows,
Deeper and brighter, alive.
She called from dreams;
It stings like the stars.
Then in the silent distance
I hear Beauties, hearts not far.

Sun Flows

On the valley's slant,
Two kangaroos in love chew grass,
Lotuses slowly close with the day,
Venus pricks a hole like glass.
Kookaburras laugh at the evening,
Sitting in trees that silently breathe.
Have you love that encompasses foundation,
Or even a peek to believe?

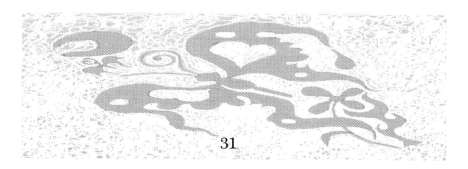

A Prey's One Second of Empathy

What comes to me in this silence
Beyond breathing wilderness?
Beyond their communications
And their instinctual fears?
Truly balanced to feed,
I sense the remorseless curse,
The merciless attack on the gentle,
As the grand meek eyes flee unrehearsed.

Tuning a Twin Soul Zen

You spoke a spark so timeless
That awe spilt my speech,
Soaked a seed and grew
The fruit of the sweetest fire.
In an empress's serenade,
One tastes the forever ocean's ebb,
Melting away sheltered silhouettes,
Drowning shyness as destiny weds.

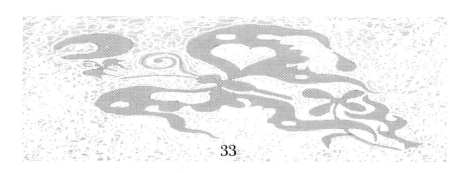

<u>*With*</u>

That moment of imperfection—
It slid down my soul.
I mingled with the barely conscious
And became whole.
A habit in habitat,
Deciphered desire,
A broken tooth and a cracked egg
Birthed a change in the illusions of a liar.

Left Wisdom

I wait, surfaced;
The ripples moved me.
Are we going down
To the sea to see what we can see?
Salty tastes linger sharply,
Yours with the breeze and in the water.
My ancestors are dust,
But that they swirl me is what matters.

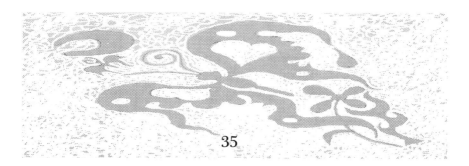

Felt

In this perfect moment of peace,
I hear droplets crash leaves,
This sharpness spaced vastly
Like new thoughts becoming truth.
In the deep pond of mind,
Ripples vibe to the surface,
Then sink to the bottom of my heart,
Silently in their within, who deserves us?

Dangle Floating

Your soft little song
Skinny dipped in my brain.
Swirl me
And then drift again,
Smile as wide as the dusk.
This pink-splashed storm
Gently has flown into me,
Holding on like it's worn.

Flowing Meek

Why shadow my sun illusion?
Contentment dilates here;
This soul will not mirror bitterness.
I feel with different eyes,
I hide no wings beneath smiles,
I just breathe me.
Love this mortal intention,
Bathing the softest serenity.

Faith Full

The shy soul dreamlessly craves—
Is this a pulse or poetry?
Half my heart's in another being,
Floating in my queen of trust.
The most romantic flame
Twirls and flickers in raindrops.
Belief is eternal,
Beyond these cosmic rocks.

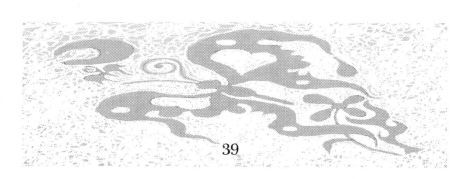

Love Sharing Our Stars

A plume of spirit,
Inertia's daydream,
Tripped from loneliness
To be found being.
The friction of fear
Tore my I,
But woke as one,
Swirling the soft souls of love this night.

Love's Elixir

The falling star grounded,
Smashing the stillness of sweet earth.
Face me, identity—
I'm not who you think I am.
I shook free the chemical illusions,
Absorbed spirit, not thought.
Have I woken something,
Feeling nothing self-taught?

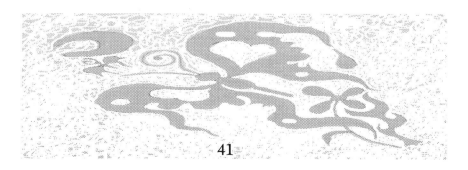

The Translucent Chrysalis

I freed it from drowning,
So it sung me a little song.
Come, we eat with the ants.
Oh, you won't live long!
The little loves on the big love,
Sparks on a poisoning rock.
The fireball swirls their lanterns
With need of a true intention to flock.

I Lay Awake, Alone

Sun-soaked chewing nature,
Sharpest tunes circle—
Where is the gardener?
This place is freedom.
I won't be tempted,
I love another.
She's my everything,
I'm nothing pretending.

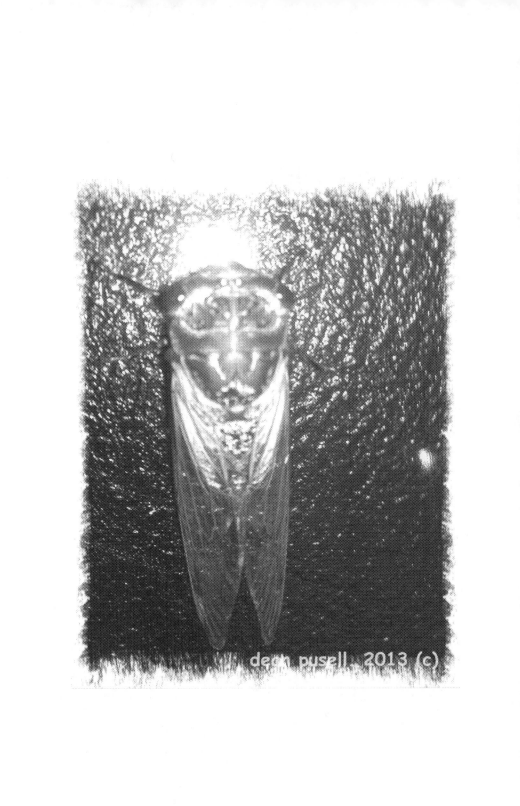

Autumn's Emotion

Heavy deciduous bitterness
Falls and leaves,
Trails my heart and blows the breeze,
Left to grieve.
Now lighter and so spacious,
Holding freedom closer than air.
Kiss me, bright starlight
Wrapped in another beauty, shared.

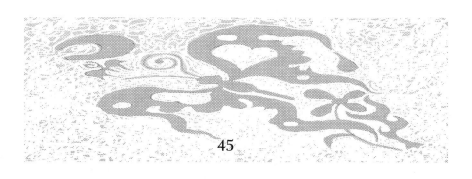

A Little Herbal Epiphany

Strings of smoke reached my sub-conscience,
In there a quiet reality,
Whispering small, delicate, spiralling truths
Of an ego's fragility.
The kingfisher squawks me awake:
Drop what you want here,
Give what you need,
Be loved, be love, me, from fear.

Don't Mind

Dawn's bright lights on your heart,
Chirping a forest of fresh warmth.
Change from being asleep,
Change again from me.
Dusk, this limited mind cries,
I want attention circling my soul.
You dreamt me, I'm here?
Me, you, I—thought we were whole.

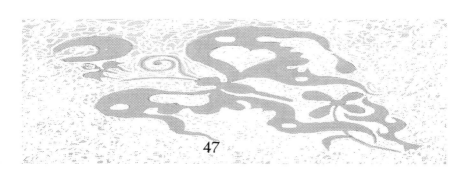

Are You Ours?

This deeply naked spirit
Holds nothing but breath and awe;
The thoughts are stillness
As the stars are waking.
Come share this flame—
We will build it to seek;
Like love's eternal fire,
The natural light glows so meek.

Blunt the Shadows

There's a flame in the corner
Flickering a little dance.
Go downwind with your lies;
You're starving our freshness.
I'll help you dig and heal
To regain the treasured light;
To be a soul keeper
Empathies your site.

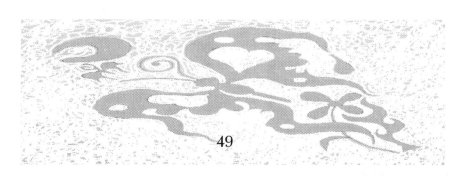

The Twilight Melt

Feel I'm bleeding dry, awaiting you.
Not my love that drains,
But my loneliness.
Your voice keeps me sane.
Quenching these heart roots softly,
Unexplainable vibes absorb new growth;
I'll never forget the sweetest spirit
That made my soul and face smile.

A Dawn's Sparkle

The gentlest absorption
Rippled me whole.
How many dreams left,
Till everything is sold?
Like glass shattering down a staircase,
The birds chime on,
Little songs sung
In a majestic passion.

Rising Smiles

At the sound of raindrops
Our hearts kindled,
Sparking a fresh love,
Together embracing the ember.
Such soft silence
Bathes the flame, gently real,
Empowers the dual spirits
As one to feel.

Dry Wings

Spit the corrupt venom,
Suck deep the mountain breeze,
Awake in this moment,
Bring smiles that please.
If I mirror the stranger's gesture,
And I welcome another's truth?
No longer feeling exiled of spirit,
Befriend the smile to you.

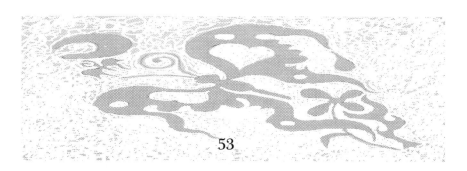

Smiling Conscious

Cloud juice cleansed my thoughts,
From fire-water lost
To melting awake,
All growing to meaning.
I fast slow this dawn,
Appreciating our feast;
Always tastes better with your heart
Sharing a candlelight of peace.

Inquiring Curiosity

Imagine a malleable, supple mind:
When one transforms within,
The external changes will bind,
Then true alignment lives to begin.
Ego's conditioned autopilot
Made the seer short;
I want a child's reference,
Like the first time purities caught.

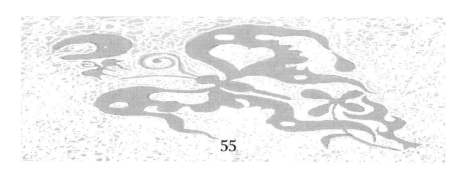

Sky Rocks

Only a hard mind breaks,
Fragments in anger,
Tames thoughts fluidly,
For then peace will linger.
During the day when sun lights the moon,
It burns me,
So I shift my shadow
To seek how imperfectly I see.

Pretty Human

Are we all not yoked together in time,
Carcasses crawling to pleasures,
A self-perpetuating animal conscience,
Existing for insatiable treasures?
Let go of those bank$,
Flow with the tides,
Smile bravely at high and low,
Don't be like the many who hide.

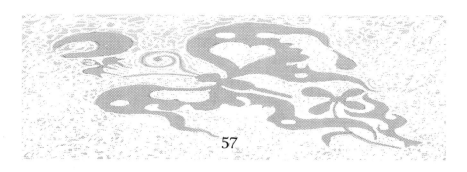

Gliding Time

A pair of wind-riding eagles
Swirl the thermo breeze.
Screaming, they dive,
Landing on the shiny serpents.
No time to shed
Or hide in dreams.
Wake to the abundance of now,
Living the beauty that gleams.

Pick Me Out of Me

The ego of silence apparently knows me.
Interpreting my light, I believed more;
This quest is so changing,
Teaching a purpose, adored.
Float, little scribbled thought,
And circle ballooned.
I felt like I'm waiting
While we're all marooned.

The Inner Rainbow

My mind aches for attention,
One of many ping's.
She blessed me a magic;
Sunlight parted our silence.
Her aura's warm in truth,
Not a quivering light.
You brought me back the soul-fire,
Illuminating a tribal sight.

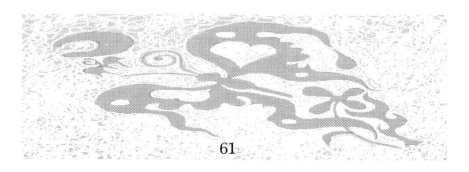

A Thought of Lightning

Dragonfly eyes drift the lilies,
Kaleidoscopes dance in the reflections,
The centre of a scented lotus
Was hit by a rainbow.
Nestled into the soft atmosphere,
Colours splash and drift.
Thunder shakes this valley,
But only my conscience did shift.

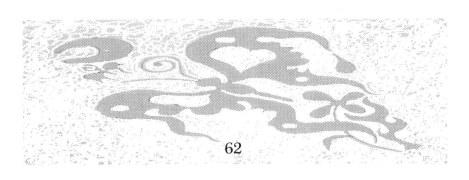

A Soul Of Irreplaceable Time

She's motivated violence;
How weak.
She's damaged the child mirror;
Now seek.
Beauty's splashed everywhere,
It's dripping and regrowing.
Where's your home,
Or does it need sowing?

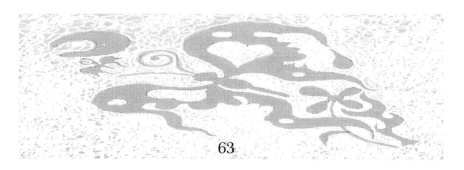

Beyond Optimism's Beauty

Is the moon a heart's pulse?
Waves vibe to the sure,
In the breeze all our breaths
Feeding the trees a little more.
While I'm here awakening dreams,
I'll appreciate this divine show.
Yes, I believe we are no mistake,
Because your pretty heart taught me so.

You Hurt

You warned you'd shoot.
I listened, but you still left.
My heart couldn't make you stay;
Now you just live in my dreams.
I revenged all for you vocally,
Like you were here.
My brothers and my sisters of trust,
I'll love like my time's near.

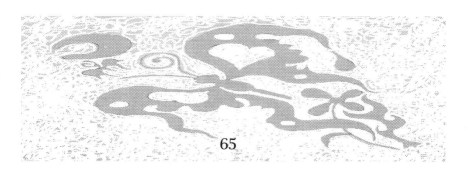

Watching a Blue Butterfly

As the sage burns,
The heaviest scent flows.
I may support no wings,
But I'll soar.
You dream, too?
Want to come?
Heart listening is the map,
And love is the fuel of the drum.

Doing to Being

Clothed in this illusion named future,
I pulled the right thread
That unveiled this new insight,
From blind to fed.
Want fell to the floor,
Stuttering on about I need it,
But in a shallow depth
Only desire believed it.

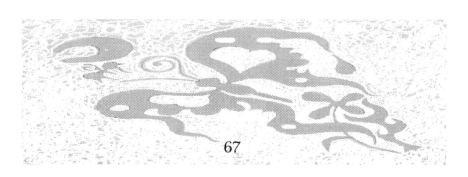

Together One Sparkle

Across the ocean and jungle,
I'll await you alone, princess.
Though we dwell dimly shy,
Our love emulates the suspended stars.
The moon's like our God
Amongst the other lovers of light.
We'll try not to fall,
Unless it's in love this night.

Raven-Haired Soul

All feelings swarm to longing
As the surface of dripping time
Distorts our reflections.
How I crave her heart.
I can scream but she's further,
I could fly but I'll wake.
Bliss feels I love her,
Deciphering intentions that I make.

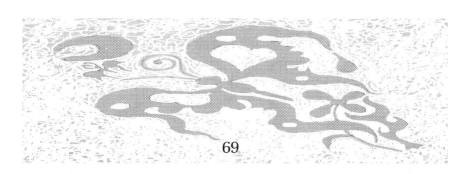

One Heart, Two Smiles

You left empty of beat,
Sweet music and my heart.
The sun's out but it's so cold;
Your soul was that shined.
Sometimes you just love,
Beyond touch and wisdom,
So let our spirits flow
In the blessing of this season.

Sprinkling Peace

Dusk is floating away softly
As the fire-globe gently drifts.
My queen of smiles
Sighs further than an echo.
Tonight her shackle of silver hearts
Mirrors the starlight;
As her soul steered a dream,
It woke this being beyond sight.

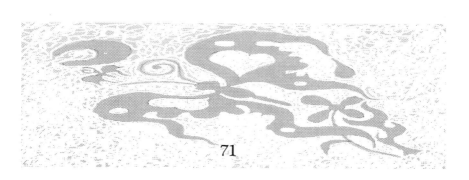

One Us

Teach me, baby,
To release the liars.
I'm sailing innocent,
Drifting your sinking truth.
You trust my conscience
Anchored in your hope?
Together one pulse
Twines our faith rope.

Drift Shimmering

A crack in the whole,
Splitting to a smile.
Is your heart sleepy?
Wandering time.
A carriage of persistent intrigue
Trickles your veins,
Even in your heart's home of imperfection,
Your pure intention still reigns.

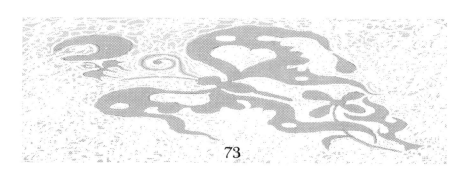

Exiled Mortality

Like a ripped butterfly,
Twirling I reflect.
I pant, open-eyed,
Fearing to love.
Your heart's safe,
She grins to light,
But I can't fly,
So she carries my soul tonight.

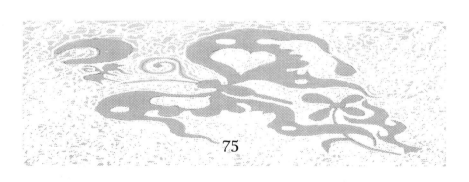

You Feel Two?

Right yourself, just a scratch;
Bite yourself, awake again.
Amongst stars and eyes,
Strangers become friends.
Two beats of growth
Hold each other's smiles,
Never meant to fall in love.
Be my one beyond the dials.

The Battle of Being

The soft turquoise flower of our wilderness,
You vibe heavily ambient,
Quivering like you're three-quarters asleep,
Splashing your unique scent.
Or is this a dream?
The I, held in the reflection—
Is it the mind that fights this heart,
Trying to conquer perception?

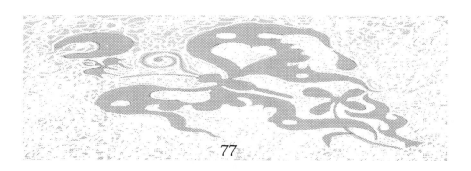

The Horizon of Bliss

I spilt your love on me;
It soaked into my veins,
It fell into my heart.
Then I, in love, fell again.
Don't crave me, widowed loneliness,
For the one grows like light.
She shines out my smiling eyes
And brings my dreams to flight.

Ghost Craves

Whom does your heart call the loudest,
Or even just echo every day?
Do they bring smiles?
Do they like invisible kisses?
Does your soul crack being apart,
But bathe healed, seeing them?
Just be thankful you're one,
Blessed in a timeless Zen.

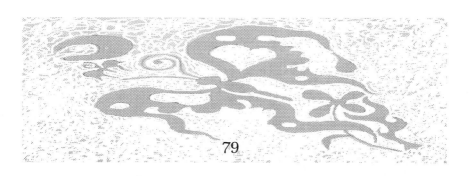

Sanctuaries of Trust

She woke to the third-eyed kiss,
Unshackled from dreams.
The soft winter sun
Floats the illuminating mystery.
Tattoos and lip prints gloss on,
Trailing the warm heartbeats.
We, the divinely synchronised,
Drumming as one repeats.

Springs Reflections

Can her soft feelings replenish?
When a scorched question blisters,
I beg time hastens;
This heart, it breathes heavy.
I suffer a want,
Though delivered the need.
I adore the princess so meek,
Her love a waking seed.

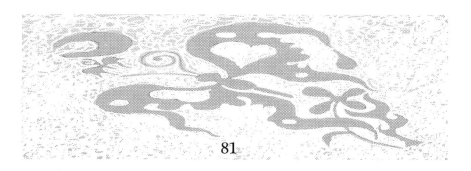

Sanctified Naturally Sacred

Softly in this coldness,
The sun sinks slowly into the earth.
I light a flame
For your heart's sight.
I wandered the shallows this dusk
And found no depth;
Nothing nestles the mind
Like embracing your next breath.

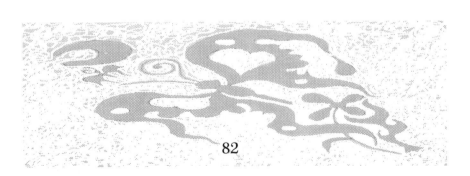

Love's Panacea

Are you the palatable placebo?
Watching butterflies and leaves falling,
Floating and fluttering,
Then twisting to life.
If ever is to be grounded,
Dig till your dreams are unearthed,
For this mortal knitted trap
Won't hold this light birthed.

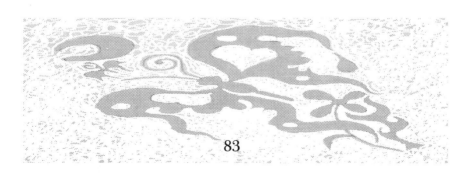

The Wide-Eyed Flourish

Eye tripped with the lightning—
I think I'm here?
Growl, cranky monstrous cloud,
Love your juice.
Sighted with my own heart
Where the rainbow fell;
I thought they were wings,
But she was dancing where she did dwell.

A Fragrant Dream

All I hear are wild birds,
Yet I crave your voice.
The sunlight sprays me,
But it's not your touch.
The golden jungle girl,
Hidden from eyes not heart,
Like the pink perfumed lotus,
Will surface a scent not far.

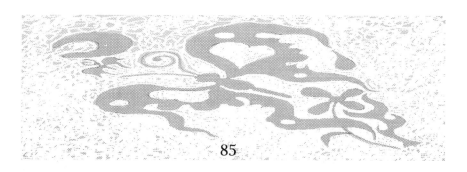

Crawling to Wings

Living a suicidal binge,
I dream to discontinue,
The softest sign broke light,
Her smile of honesty.
So now till loves discipline,
I've left the me for him,
The newest metamorphosis,
Hence the will begins.

Doctor Albert Hofmann's Medicine

Scratch this to dirt,
I'm sleeping tomorrow.
Little heartbeats everywhere,
Living their favourite song.
Leave me alone with you;
We sway in a dream,
Growing this sixth sense.
From ego I wean.

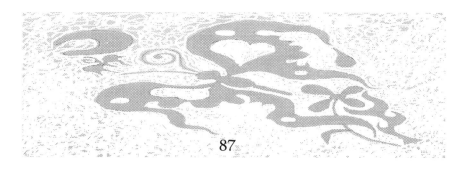

A Lunar Bliss
of Fire and Stars

Orange sparks rocketed the moon,
Bouncing off the glow
Trickling down to my heart,
And sparkling me with warmth.
A forest of silhouettes do wrap and mesh,
In the truth before I dream,
And you, the dawn that awakes the I,
Always make love believe.

Two Souls Chant

The ambient gaze embedded,
A sight softer than the flesh of a rose.
It threw me to smiles
Of a breathless float.
A whirlpool of earthy, chocolate brown eyes—
Swirling, I fell in her heart.
Silence blew a whisper:
Welcome to love

The Silent White Drum

Through the broken branches
She shines softly;
The lunar bewilderment
Magnetises my soul.
Illuminate me fearless,
As only love can.
I melt back into her heart;
This time of moon is no dream.

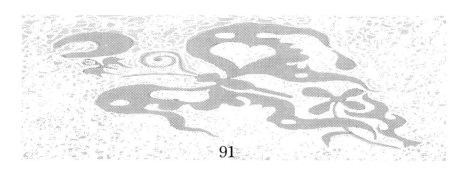

Promise I'm Awake

My golden empress so earthed,
Dreamt smiling beneath the crystal stars.
She found her heart breathing
And lay it softly back inside.
Like a breeze to a flame,
I call to her in dreams,
Then I find
I'm in love, reality.

The Sane Fear

Bigger than flesh, this energy,
Awake more than I've seen.
Read more beyond this realm,
Take leash of that dream.
The sun's time rotisseries so slowly,
Look a spray of rocks and a flame.
Your enlightenment is Zen,
When peace is beyond the clock.

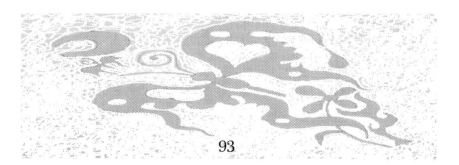

Sparks in Meat

What's discovered intently gentle,
Sometimes in an unseen nature,
Sometimes an unfelt love?
Has it all been sent to test you?
What if the omnipotents are real?
Did you exhibit a light of significance?
Though dwelling in the darkness under the sun,
I believe we're a choice to consequence.

<u>Harmony Heals</u>

When a creature births near you,
We grow together,
We dream alike,
And sometimes lose a feather.
Always help the flight of happiness;
Never forget your nest.
Love has many shelters,
But unconditional loves the best.

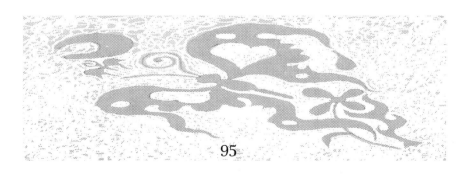

A Broken Cage

I venture while she dreams.
Which realm's the illusion?
Three eyes in sunlight
Have shone a new truth.
You see two reflections utter,
Friends of fondness for an honest zeal;
They conceived a trust so pure,
The language was to feel.

Naked Being

My silence bears responsibility.
I did glimpse clarity;
Perfection taught me I'm sorry,
That I should give not as a rarity.
The view from the gardens a cosmic chasm
That stops no growth in me,
Mortal angels do exist;
They hugged me deliberately.

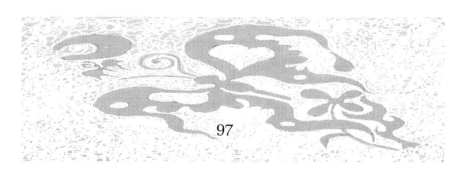

Modernising Nature

Don't feed me—I'll lose the instinct to seek.
Awaken me; I don't need to dream.
Why doze on the earth?
Footprints are clean.
A wind of wet salt trickles my emotions,
Down to a pained heart.
Why a toxic existence?
Love is the system to start.

Align the Noise

We're told if you hear voices,
You're a crazy being.
But what if you hear one—
The higher self opening to a new seeing?
We'll I'm keeping him;
We sync uniquely,
I think I earned him.
Or maybe he saved me discretely?

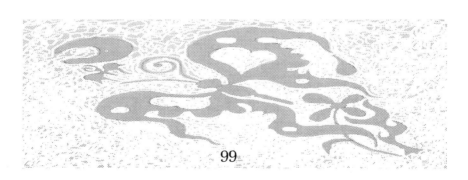

Denounce the Lenses

Induce your dynamics
By living in appreciation,
For the inevitable magnetism
Will flow a new tuned strength.
The happiest essence here
Is a sharing being.
Erase blind judgement and give all love;
Every spirit has meaning.

She Sways Like a Flower

I love that you don't lie,
Even if all you had was an hour.
Don't hide your pretty song;
I saw what your smile cocooned.
You stargaze like a child,
As your soul restlessly surfaces.
You'll never be a butterfly, '
Cause you're an angel in bloom.

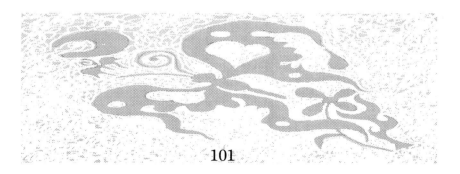

<u>Energy Drifts</u>
<u>the Gem of Silence</u>

Are you learning from the edge?
Be patient for the stillness,
Four seasons heal and pass,
Change is so sacred.
Now you in that mirror knows,
Rippling thoughts can be a mask,
There's a treasure beneath the concealment,
The largest jewel is the smile you bask.

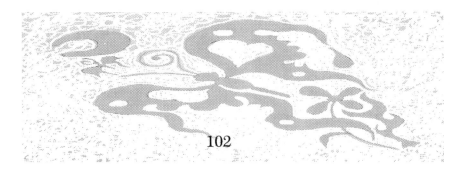

A Circular Echo

Learn to be alone,
You were told in this sun,
I soared 'cause you listened
Beyond the sensory of numb.
A wisdom so mattered,
In hair and spirit,
Your journey's a smile
That coexists with the belief to conceive it.

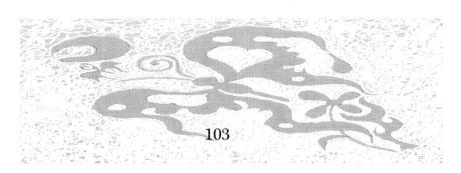

jean rusell / 2013 (c)

A Twilight's Night Shade

A speck of silver
Pierces back from the stars.
She glides beside me
In a perfumed heart.
My mind slid like dusk—
The moon was ours,
Above an oasis quenched,
And rained on the flesh we housed.

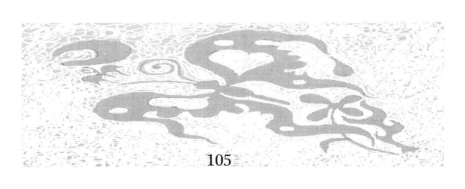

Squinter

So awake it hurts,
But I see colour in the distance.
I dog paddle dreams,
Smiling without resistance.
Around me they stand drowning;
I throw hope without holes,
But you don't surface
To the light of the souls.

Scratching a View

Shivering fatigues me;
As the bubble rises,
I blast a deafening thought,
Life has so many prices.
Guess they're dead wings?
But that's not a mask,
So we breathe as one
In a mortal dusk.

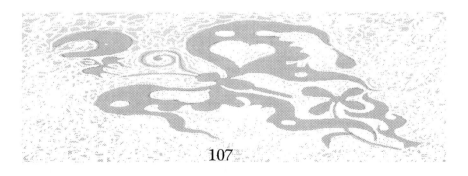

Awakening the Zen Slumber

Out of my head,
Your trespassing thought;
I guess it's had meaning?
From the melted sign it distorts.
I breathed a ylang ylang flower,
And it vibes me fresh—
Love for everyone
On this planetary nest.

I'm Waiting Fear

I recognise you,
Me of melted mirror.
You really need this?
No.
Come, gorgeous lesson,
I'm alive again.
Hold my heart,
More than same.

Two Trip Time

I lost it all—
You, me,
Body, light,
Twirled in comprehensive.
Is this planetary dream,
Now back to life?
Appreciate what seems
Us on earth's mortal flight.

Conscious on a Stone

Your kiss stole my dream,
Prising awake to the prettiest face.
Without wings she awaits,
Explaining in a soft gleam.
Something is peeling the orange dusk;
Then the wind blew in the stars.
I smell sweet strings of nectar drift.
Being love has no surpass.

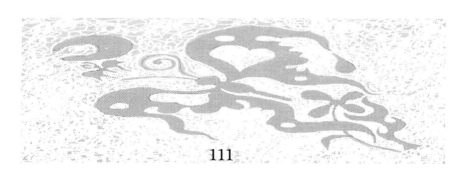

In a Storm
of Divine Opportunity

The cotton clouds are leaking,
The suns in the egg.
You wander in your dreams too?
Given a light without a tear of begging.
Keep the smiles strong;
Vibes are like the breeze,
Free to refresh,
No price or a lease.

Rented Empathy

That's not who I knew—
The kaleidoscope imploded.
Who'll memorise the snare
If your heart's demoted?
A wise universal shard of truth
Speaks the believing dreamer,
Blasts the dark with light,
Synchronising to clarity's aura.

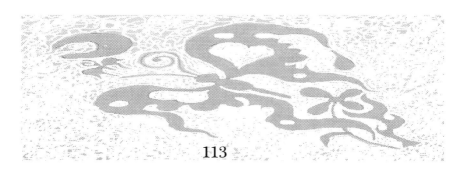

A Draft in a Draft

The gentleness of peace sways on me.
As reflections separate rippled,
I know what enlightens myself:
It flows through tripled.
This awakened consciousness,
 Journey's the heart of intention.
Clocks are too fast,
Feelings must be released from detention.

Faith's Moon

Bound by objects,
There's a quarter moon,
A soul on a rock
Breathing a tune.
Little babies can see what we see,
As we follow their innocent ways.
Children live in the now,
Feeling the moment stays.

Toxicity Deprogrammed

Songs smash into songs,
Insects scratch at the breeze.
The red desert—
It nourishes and it bleeds.
A number of spirits question
The concrete evidence.
Our light dims to machinery;
The answers are in tribal existence.

Attitude's Belief

I'm shown the ugliness
Of what not to be;
Excess is dangerous.
This one smiles within sacred sanity.
We're all a magical vibe,
Radiating at different speeds,
Then connected to absorbing at this life,
For empowering emotional feeds.

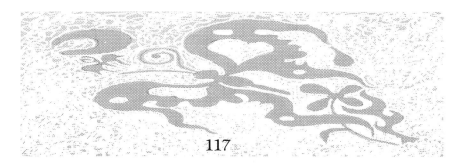

Chic Chalet

As old as existence,
Rain trickled the forest,
Surrounded by the living melody
Many heartbeats did confessed.
Love the cleansing droplets,
To bathe and drink,
So they sing a little louder,
For your happiness is what you think.

The Grey Chameleon Changed

Did a lie fade you
And drain all your brightness?
You climbed from their plague
As they bleached you from kindness.
The zing of your androgynous mind
Forever holds a balanced love.
The tears bought a rainbow,
Patiently reflecting the colours from above.

Freed a Wise Vibe

The ambiguous sanctum
Birthed a beautiful lesson:
Smiles are precious,
As so are mistakes of confession.
A perfect meaning
Is fearless to wither,
Empathies a diamond,
Makes all lights quiver.

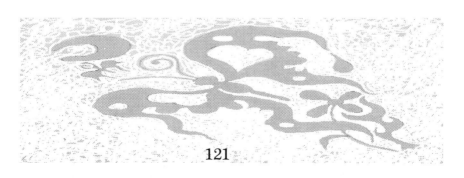

Interviewing Intention

Defuse to a quaint,
Inspect but don't cling,
Feel not a prey to fault,
Foster the intuitive to sing.
Strengthen the shelter of tenderness,
Radiate the welcomed sincere.
Are you unaware of your healing
By freeing a stranger from fear?

Approaching Eve's Sleep

A water dragon runs at me, famished,
Beasts stomp and crack leaves,
Central nervous system shuts down.
I feed the dragon some fire-bugs that bleed.
Screeching cockatoo's hover
Like anxiety's madness scratching,
I grew this for you;
Now a tree house is waiting.

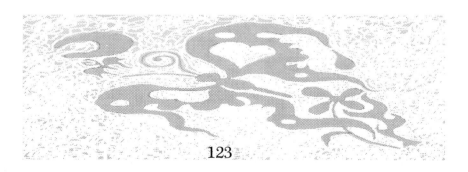

Analytically Evolving Within

What a storm;
Think it sunburnt my face.
Fear is an illusion,
Like the cast of a gooseberry.
This comfortable veil will perish,
Exchanging change for time,
Slower but wiser on purpose.
Your heart will have a new rhyme.

A Sloth Suicide

This vehicle's no home,
 Just a large husk.
Toss the poisons,
Your temples scorched.
You know I once saw you alive?
Fearing this fake replica that blinds,
You knew your centre would drown—
Your choice to spiritually define.

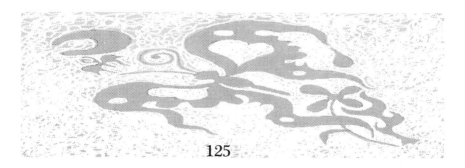

<u>Mortalities Deliverance</u>

I'll wait for your dried essence;
The knees of nectar stone the hive.
Land now, honey,
And shed your golden find.
The sweetest selflessness
Groups love,
Sharing potents best,
Where being syncs above.

The Freshest Quench

Come dry your wings
In the deity's breeze.
Where do you drip from?
Your eyes?
So the weight of sadness
Anchors your flight,
But now we breathe deep
And follow the heart's sight.

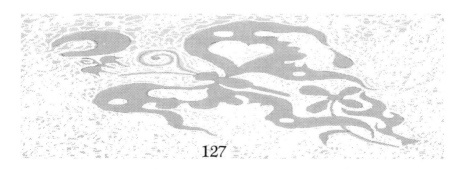

Meek Deep

Through these seeking eyes,
Life soaks my heart;
Beauty then flows to a smile,
And there the ripple can start.
My heart's like a child's tree house,
Swaying in expansion.
I don't need darkness to see;
There's a ladder of light in love's enchantment.

Innocently Awake

Are you vapour or a light,
Or is it intricate mud?
The coolest winds flow;
This drying shelter starts to crack.
A piercing little light
Reveals blue eyes.
What's inside the human shrine
That the unconsciously devolved deny?

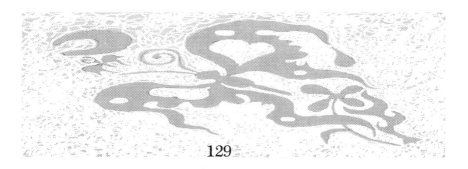

Now a Dripping Dusk

The lake sparkled like crushed diamonds.
I'm scribbling in the rain;
My mouth tastes like native honey,
Breathing the awe of the mountains.
Like a rotten blanket the clouds hung,
Stretched heavily and ripped,
As a passing kingfisher screamed.
The sweetest rain I sipped.

A True Seek

Swiftly the colours were taken.
The cold winds threw attitude,
Loved the cosmic trip
Of our honesties being nude.
 If you forget your roots, you'll fall,
 So respect all lives beneath our sun.
 I love what we're given:
 The option to treat all harmlessly as one.

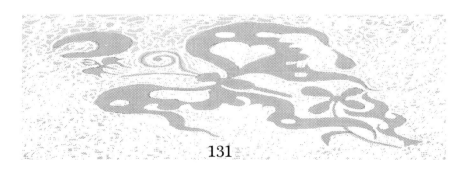

A Tear-Drop of Meek Harmony

I'm sad till I hear your voice.
You're my friend,
Welling my blurred, glassy eyes,
Waiting.
The bravest being,
Beyond corruption.
My honest light,
I delve your flame.

Encompass Healing

Do you have a flame of awareness,
Or is it a smouldering sleep?
I'm here with you this time;
Give this fire to the weak.
I love our elements with respect;
They nurture us to smiles,
Show love to the hungry and cold,
For that peace of strength travels miles.

Watching Water Fowl

In the movement of a shadow,
I fall to a dream.
When will I fully wake?
Like a bursting bubble bleeds,
Trickling the serotonin of belief,
Sincerity is our only power.
They're selling our garden rock—
 Now it's unnaturally drowning sour.

See You in Them

You wear your hurt
Over your mask,
And through your tired mind
You carry a body sculpted truth.
As a sound human whole,
We speak more than we think,
Rise beyond esteem,
And love the lost that sink.

A Dusk with Poppies

The raven crackles behind me
As the sun seethes;
A machine drags its blades,
And the road kill bleeds.
Too fast this pace,
Permitted free on weekends,
Yet poverty tries to drown you enslaved,
With a cost of the bends.

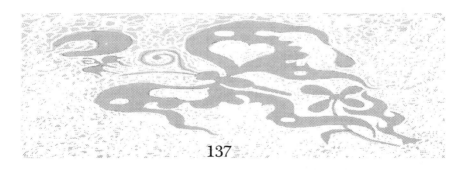

Bullet in the Baby Crib

This intense air is eating at me,
But would I return naive?
I've seen so much, I'm not
Too shocked to comprehend the human.
Swirled in a curse of gestures,
Yet this lantern loves.
We're one together;
Time to drop the hate guns.

Love's Adoption

Is that another shamanistic dream?
Aerial views painted like glass
With symbols sprinkled,
All now unmasked.
Breathe as one; we'll go higher
Till our vibe is light,
Or just be the quenched love
To their orphaned site.

Observing the Crave

What if she's the one?
My dream sent signs;
I ache at the clock,
But learn what binds.
In stillness I heard the trees breathe,
Then with a breeze through the leaves,
I felt for her again,
Living an emotional tease.

Floating Appreciation

Winging the nectar fuel,
The butterfly tongues a flower,
Bouncing the air like a dream—
Or is this?
So if we all do dream together,
Why would we fight?
 If we wake this day a dream—
That's us alive.

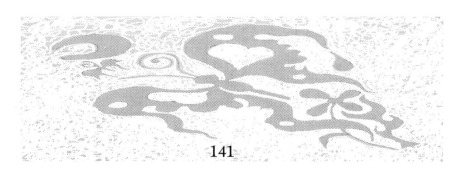

Bumblebee Bliss

As dusk melts slowly to diamonds,
The golden forest leaves to dream.
My fire brings back the trees,
Splashing it woven.
Hear the river trickle over stones?
As this mind sounds of dragonfly,
I really saw a bumblebee being itself,
Free as an eagle's cry.

Ylang Ylang Dream

Sciatica's scream at the dusk,
The softest black bats river from mountains,
Their clock is the sun,
Returning before a new cycle.
A trail of ash
Follows the quiet mutter
As lightning creates the opal.
You are my unique brother.

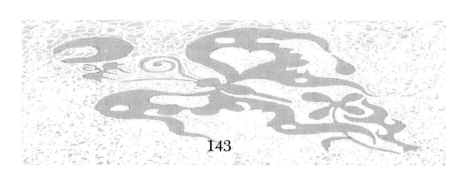

A Droplet Inspired

The sky"s song
Crashes and rolls like surf;
It smashes with lights fast,
And a tree cracks fire.
A serpent slid the rain,
Shedding on cold.
So change does flow on,
Living fresh as three-fold

Broken Puppets

How do you see yourself?
Surviving to a true shine?
Needing to abandon a life enslaved?
Blooming a fresh mind?
Some systems are such a lie,
Creating hopeless drones.
Be an intention of love;
 It's your heart's home.

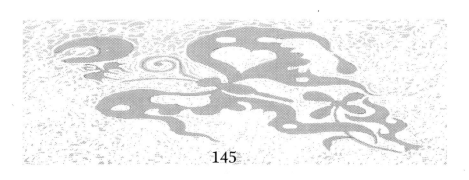

A Matter of Being in Breath

The curse and the cure
Exist together,
Biting and healing,
Tumbling for belief.
I've seen dead,
A broken lantern and flame,
Back to clay and stone.
So live, don't blame.

Climb Clarity

Welcome, shelter here;
This heart listens with empathy.
Raindrops and stars swept,
Cleansing me to smile.
I think I'm breathing slower,
Bellowing a thought.
We rise, we fall,
But unfortunately some live bought.

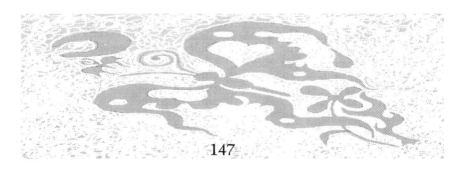

Grow, Don't Suffer

Under an eagle,
Next to a seed,
I'm here,
I bleed.
Breathe to heal,
Never is intention illusion.
My space within
Respects life's contusions.

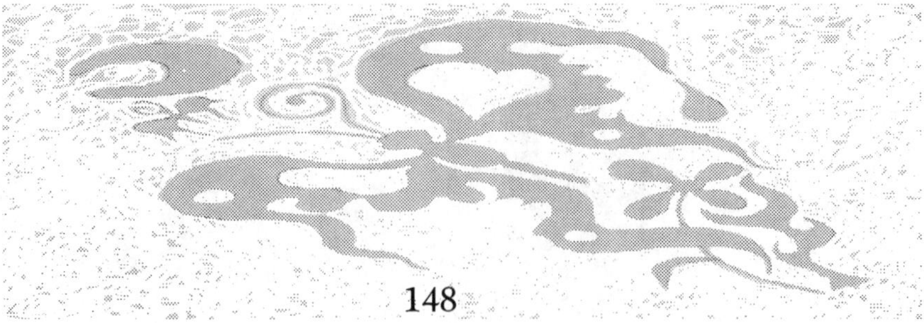

Jean pusell, 2013 (c)

Who's Program?

In windy, wet reflections
I trip;
Belonging to illusions,
I strip.
Shedding shallow scars
Like summer's tree,
Bathing in dusk's fire rock,
I'm smiling, learning me.

Chemical Compass

You dragged my voice slow;
I echoed for land,
I tasted the numbness of winter
And tripped in Gods hand.
We float on this rock
Amongst glowing stones.
Now I echo alone,
Seeking my heart's home.

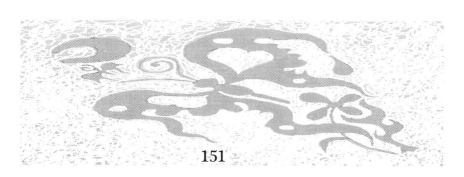

Heal Yourself amongst the Stars

My neighbour is hiding herself
Like an iris at light speed'
Dissolving, she's teething the mind gaps,
Escaping anxiety's need.
Your light visited to heal her,
But unsatisfied with your answer,
That love could have realigned her precious heart.
Sadly her choices became her cancer

The Depth Ripples

That blister's not from that light;
She didn't mean to burn me.
I dreamt your consequence
And healed in your eyes.
My heart's no desert;
I believe in soul.
No one is meat,
The value unfolds.

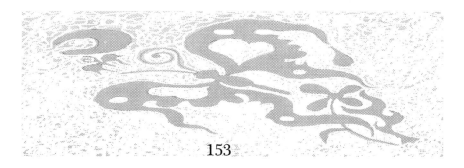

Alight in the Oneness

In the moonlight an eagle cried;
Thunder rolled like surf,
Dumping the silence
As a seedling births from its shell.
Guess it's real?
Though serene as a dream,
So the sensory unravelled
To absorb my belief.

Dreamy Silhouettes

Quivering blades swirling the surface
Beneath the ponder of thought;
In perfume the lotus opened
To dwell amongst the distorted.
Breathing the essential quiet breath,
Vividly I splashed from a dream.
Nature has this peaceful effect,
To accept gently the foreseen.

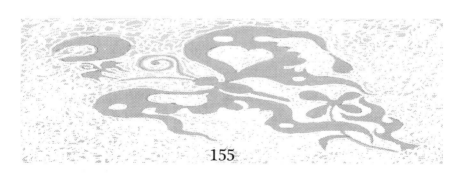

Cardiac Pollination

I resisted this day;
It was a haunt of past recognitions.
But then this alone lotus opened,
Shining with the water's ambition.
In silence she closed with dusk
Like a stoned dream.
Lily pads broke raindrops;
Now to cleanse from self
I must wean.

Earthing to Spirit

From the stretching shadows I found sun.
The light embraced me;
This being's intensely alive
Apparently.
This button works,
My peyote visionaries.
The succulent hidden realm
Deciphers the necessary.

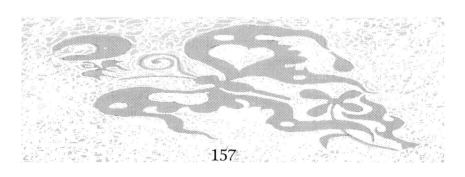

Landing to Live

Can you feel for more than yourself?
It pierced the light and scratched the sky,
From seed to tree, like a heart.
Never let empathy die.
Swim to the sure,
In sane safety.
Life's a butterfly's dream,
And illusions are only tasty.

Uniting a Light's Loyalty

Bliss is right of the sun,
Dreaming harmless,
Waking to signs,
Travelling smiles.
Hope balances the edge,
But if we fell,
We'd trust in our grasp;
It's in the roots that we dwell.

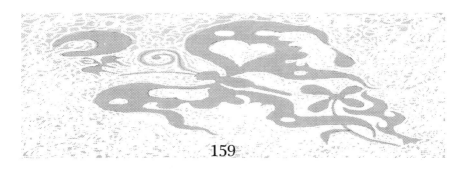

Micro in a Marco Fluxation

Drinking dried herbs stone me grounded.
Anticipation screams a roost;
Sage perches me in a darkening dusk,
Surrendering to these lunar diamonds.
The cosmic sparkles,
Blasts and falls
Like a being's emotions,
Refreshing me to small.

Smiling Home

Happiness fell soft,
Less than a feather
But deeper than a dream,
Deciphering together.
Let's just feel
In the beats of honesty.
As the mind surrenders,
Your heart will come to me

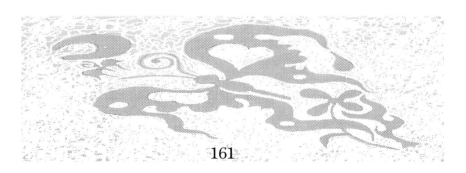

Not Shore

Wandering the circle of oscillation,
Peeling back those leaves,
Feeling the whispered beat,
Intricately questioning you.
If I'm a light
And you're a meat that wants to meet,
I feel no harmony in us—
Or is this growth incomplete?

A Free Show

Chasing butterfly thoughts,
A grounding so nectareous,
Tattered it leaves,
Answered.
Fresh wind flows change Like wild honey;
A golden sweet dusk
Needs no money.

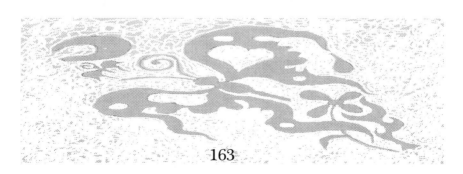

dean pasell : 2013 (c)

The Precious Sanctum

I rummaged like it's survival,
Then we listen in the shine,
The hallway's sweep a glassy moonlight,
In a soft, swaying surge.
The symbols sprout sacred
Like the flourishing dream;
Our bodies a vibrant home,
Housing the gems of being.

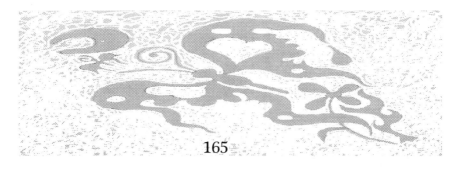

A Cleansing Scribble

The orchestration of control
Keeps this will potent.
I listen to my sighing weakness,
Then feed it a new strength.
Through the fresh filter of ears,
My mind's circuitry did spark;
It rushed unravelling to a smile,
Leaving what propagated stark.

Squint and Flint

One day I'll be gone,
And you may want to know me.
I'll just be thoughts
As you'll be lying here.
Time is a breath,
Shared and smiled,
So in this global sweep
Try to wake for a while.

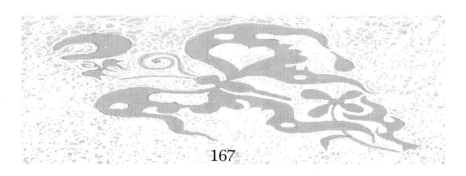

Dose

I hear you crawl;
Slithers leave no scratch.
Convince my light
You're a flame too.
Zeal held the tightest hug—
Was I there?
I truly melted;
In love's refuge we share.

A Swell Pantomime

Dripping in shiny rocks,
You still our flesh,
Gathered and woven,
A little mortal confessed.
Dream and I'll listen
As the milky clouds collide.
Inhale this moment and smile;
Life's a mystical ride.

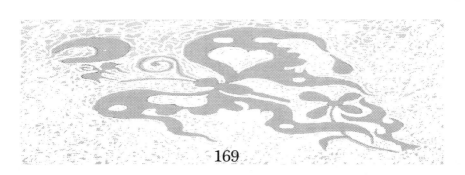

Metamorphism's a Gorgeous Transmission

In a cosmic distant chrysalis,
She feels the breeze crack her home.
In starlight the dreams awake,
Flowing her soft, wet wings.
In the resistance of suffering,
The clock of illusion taught me
Freedom is of thought
That manifests embodied.

The Bell-Birds at Dawn

Untangle that sound;
We're too big for their prey.
Come, we reconnect
Before the moon is our blue day.
The golden white suspended magnet
Centres us, we trust.
Life's so sacred. together alive,
As our beings blush.

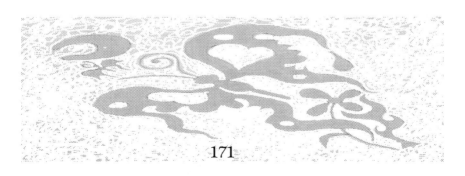

The Tranquillity Beneath

Broke off some cocoon
To help inside,
But it changed the timing
Of a natural birth.
So I've learnt in peace,
All thrive in sleep;
They're sculpting a dream
Of waking free.

Dream Conscious

So many meanings
Just dig and unfold.
Time deciphers the pieces
Till dreams glow.
Tree or pillar,
Stars or a dirty bulb,
Signs realm both mind worlds,
Your quest to solve.

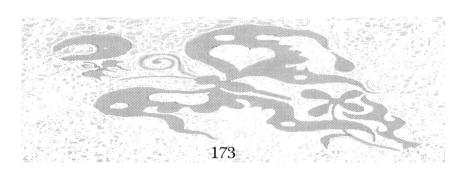

A Fresh Zest

The stone shone on my face;
I so adore just being.
From her sonic smile
I heard your love.
We all choose our life,
Lived well or cursed.
Never let the loveless defeat you
Or be rehearsed.

Magnifying the Moment

The fire above the shell,
Cracked to warmth,
Lost the cold-blooded tooth
To the new taste of change.
Smear me with the question,
How will I grow?
Fearlessly in the now,
Or fret for tomorrow to show?

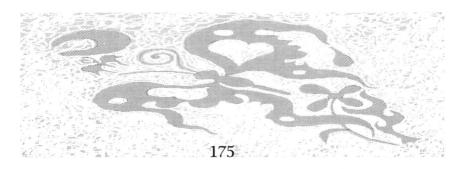

Purpose

A living wooden symbol
Showed me foundation
Truly centred—
This is creation.
From a seed to a tree,
Like from baby boy to me.
As a spirit that paths a light,
It lanterns the eternal dream.

Identity's Corpse

Drowning in the deceits of ego,
Illusions flood some of my friends.
My being's not a fashion;
This core settles to a foundation.
Forget the costume and mask
And the liquid ferments.
Serenity isn't poured into me
With a little cup of pretence.

External Meek

Is that your clock up there?
Mine the sun.
I'll wake soon,
Rather a seed than gun.
I love so close,
I never choose by colour.
Innocence is the friend
That amplifies the trust in others.

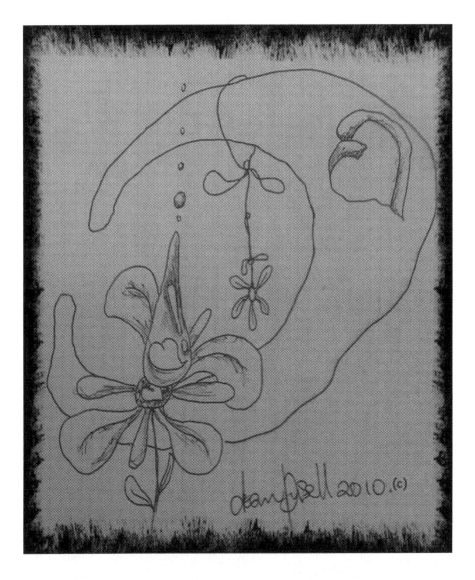

My Face Made That Puddle

I am of no speech,
For my soul, it aches,
Breathlessly saddened.
I'm lost, what my thoughts make.
A whole moon and a sun has passed;
Nothing still comforts me,
 Just emptiness until her voice.
But the tears taught me to see.

An Omnipotent Test

A mind of inner stillness
Balances the power of meditation;
Let breath connect this being
To a majestic revelation.
We are truly materials of earth,
Constructed on this tree-breathing planet,
For we are of one purpose,
But that's not the way they mean it.

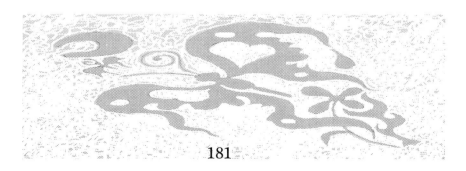

The Little One's Children

Half in the shadows,
Hit by pollen,
The world keeps sprouting,
Even if you're sullen.
We're just visitors;
You can pretend you own,
But it's just not ours.
There must be a future sacredly sown.

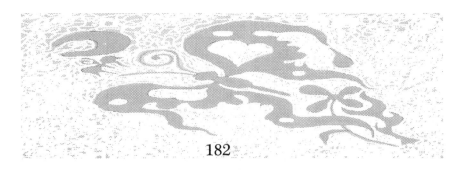

Under Skin's Garment

Come, my love, to the sacred place,
A silence in gratitude;
We dwell to manifest
A mind of the freshest altitude.
No boundary and lesser of form,
The heart of now appears/
Breathe earth's breath
And love this life sincere.

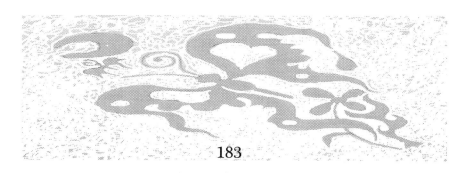

Starry

My blood is of the ocean,
My body of planet earth.
Gravitate and connect,
Smile and harmonise to worth.
Balance the universe's energy,
Synchronise our vibrations;
In feelings, movement, and thought,
We affect all of creation.

A Healing Compass

Your fear of lost paraphernalia
Is tenaciously ebbing your thoughts.
A resistor's anxiety of pain
Clings now to habitual living.
Contemplations thrive to blossom;
Follow me bewilderment.
I'll translate the invisible you,
You choose to bloom your commitment.

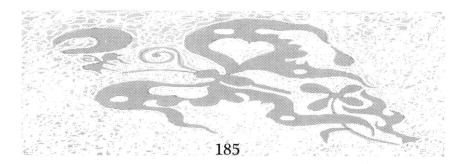

Altogether Alone in Space

Look at the time,
Dreamer of the wake.
Any more conscious,
My rest you can take.
Words stop murders,
Words bring birth.
Such a cursed existence,
But it's your choice of earth's worth.

The Childless Human Desert

My mind paddles around
As thoughts dodge like insects.
So down I'm scratching a grave,
Digging a root or some defect.
Don't know what's perfect anymore,
Safe being alone.
I'm a torn love,
Left chewed like a bone.

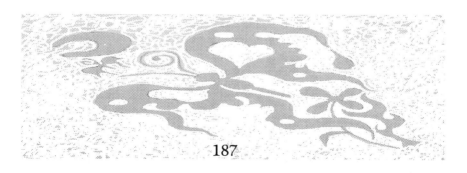

Dangerously Beautiful

So far from innocence,
Fear whispers my mind.
Here's another heart scar
Detached to soul blind.
Broken, I allowed destiny
To fix in divine time;
In all receptivity
I surrender to the sign.

From a Droplet to a Man

I see smoke,
And smell trees;
While you poison yourself,
I silently grieve.
Analyse an ancient page,
Dissolve your false identity,
Find peace as a sage,
And surrender to serenity.

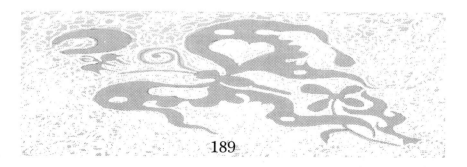

Sail from the Shell

It stretches and sheds,
A weathered-scarred skin,
Gazing, I deeply breathe the sky
To seek here where I begin.
I've grown fresh now,
My tattered, ripped costumes the past.
Life's quenched clean;
Time to raise the mast.

A Conscious Consciousness

Your eyes scream:
Silence is dumb,
I am peace,
Not evolving numb.
You go ahead;
I'm here to listen.
A silent space
Will find what glistens.

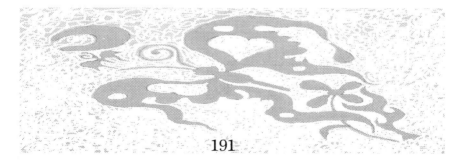

Inkling

The cruellest trinket
Takes a baby's breath.
Yes, you look nice,
Nicer than death.
How do you pretend
They don't feel?
The same heart,
But without a meal.

Feed

Pecking at the earth,
Minimalistic wage,
Black African gold,
The invisible chained slave.
Starved babies to profit,
Ignore their pain?
Look at your jewellery—
This isn't sane.

dean pusell 2013©

Three Loving Spirals

Are you a vessel of light,
Hiding unique music?
A heartbeat and a voice
Will wither if you don't use it.
Not even seldom are you stirred
To bite back at your kind.
Guide love with respect,
All intentions always return, you'll find.

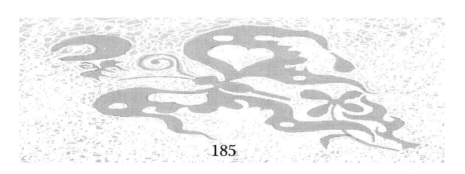

A Dawning Pilgrimage

I vanquish the temperament
To forge a conveyance
That lures and taints;
My ego died in the morning.
Tears lost in the dew,
 I live not a false promise.
This, my offering to you,
 I've peeled my subconscious.

Sprout

Aspirations of a mere visionary,
Metamorphosed to reverence—
This acceptance of us a baby to grave
Tenderly surges pure potential.
Carry no fist of ultimatum,
Keep your hand open to ones of need,
Truest freedom is choice;
We can all fall, and we all bleed.

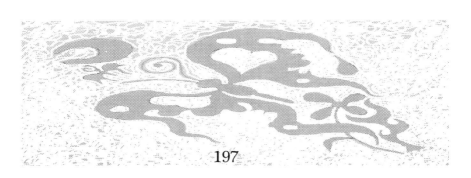

Catalytic Entropy

In this moment of fertile thoughts,
I'm earthing no symbolic attachment;
Deliberately blinded to an elusive illusion,
My ego fragments to no catchment.
More than a sting, reality throbs,
But the exchange of a waking mind's eye;
Now sweet significance is shackled,
Learning the I that I built was a lie.

Do You Bearably Cling?

Purge your impatience,
Seed a mental truth,
Entice a deep resourcefulness
Within reclaiming your purity.
Interpret the chatter,
Bless the commentary to softness;
We share the same air,
So breathe the oneness.

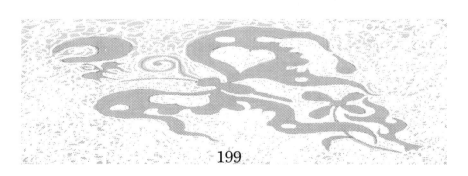

Boundary of Identities

A benevolent inquisitor
Hides not from the mystique;
A clay nest sways above lilies.
One of these three eyes did peek,
We house perfection,
We dream a little awake.
You only learn to live
When desire dies by no mistake.

Knew Angel

What a true dethronement—
You chose to suffer over illusion,
She left fingerprints on your heart
And tiny sparks of confusion.
Born last century,
I died tonight,
Grounded to dust
With a fearless insight.

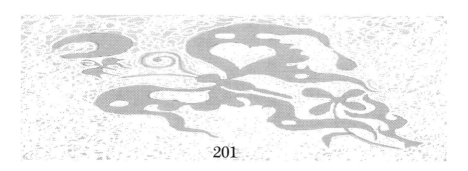

Certainly Unsure

Am I passive or ineffective?
Am I numb or at peace?
Digesting perspective,
It's a planet on lease.
Multidimensional acts of love
Dapple a dabble of integrity;
Don't block the curing,
Harness the powers of empathy.

Cocoon Splinters

Clarity's equilibrium
Energised a fresh vibe,
The wholeness of well-being—
Thirst's alive.
There's lessons in the hurt;
Buried in my meat, I hissed.
The butterfly floated freely '
Cause I opened my ancient fist.

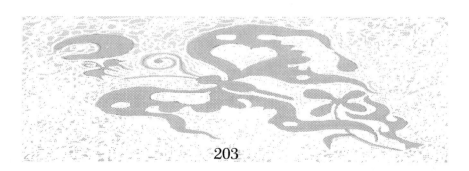

Dismount to Consequence

Be thankful for your feast,
Or you're just a mindless grub:
Chewing, sipping like a chore,
And of no comprehension to the hub.
Don't ride life to find a life;
Isn't it hunting like a machine?
Instead use harmony,
It's love that will aid the foreseen.

A Point Meant

All these lights on a rock,
Pacing these territories.
My mind shot Zen
Through a cloud to divinity.
A planet of forgetting souls,
Hiding their innocent shine.,
Earn your life, precious human,
Give another sometime.

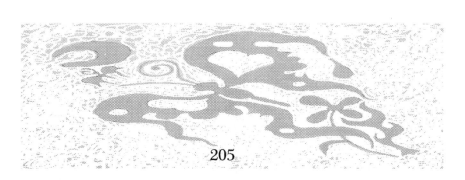

Kindle

The flutter of curiosity
Sparks a conscious ember
To flame a blazed thought:
Floating the third-eye tender.
Eloquently the tameness twinkled,
Peacefully it ushered through eyes,
Salvations in the attic
Never masquerading the soul's tie.

Humbling Dictation

To bear the bare
Deafened by the known,
I open the soul's door;
An inner gaze was shown.
Our vehicle's our servant
Commanded by a desirable mind.
Be victor of the inner prowls of doubt
To reconnect in a child's time.

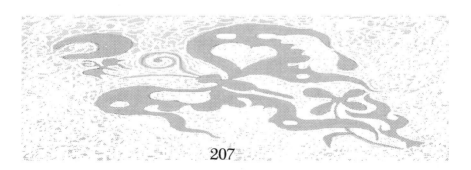

Live, Don't Rent

Liberate the noise
That swirls your theatre.
In the now I exhale those thoughts
To breathe silence nearer.
Insight to life's a symphony,
Your freedom to orchestrate.
Love is the belief
To judge not, nor discriminate.

dean pusell. 2013 (c)

Faith's Grandeur

I'm cash-less to paint;
An ink of poetry to paper will do.
Life is all I have left,
So this I will pursue.
An orange butterfly just spiralled around me,
Dancing a naive flight,
Enjoying existence now,
Unaware it has only four nights.

Angelic Eyes Vibe a Heart

I called out for her;
She travelled and found me.
No promise here tomorrow,
Then today it will be.
She's truth like a breeze,
Flowing another feeling through.
I never asked for this,
It's just what we do.

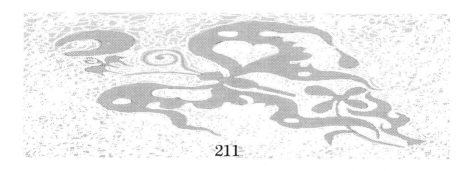

Spilt Will

I'm not just alive—
I am love.
Did I exist to satisfy my body's hunger,
Or give like a light from above?
Do not hand
What cannot be stolen.
Pleasures of the earth,
Don't tempt the spiritually evolving.

In A Minute Minute

Come, sweet butterfly,
Leave this dark cocoon.
Fear is so stagnate,
As freedom's a colourful tune.
Stretch out your pain,
Dry those shimmering wings,
Chase the rich nectar,
And flutter till your heart stings

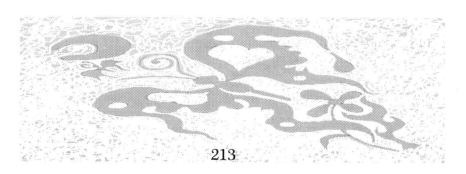

The Inhabitant's Trail

Their land is their church,
Chasing tracks to their creator.
Take only what's needed
So nature can replenish later.
Never another shall starve
Or die unloved;
They cherish this life alive
And worship the abundant light above.

Purifications Energy

Softer than perfume,
Sweeter than mountain air,
My beloved voice
Melts me there.
There is my centre
Of feelings and dreams.
I've never loved another the same—
Now I know what this means.

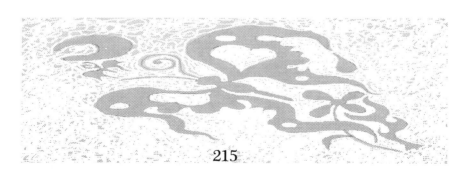

Trust Ripples Hope

Who's down there?
No, below the surface.
Your bubbles hit me
Like a gentle karma.
Look up, here's my hand,
I'll pull you free.
It's not bad being saved;
Sometimes it's destiny.

Surge

Mortality reminded me
I'm flightless tonight.
She's that way,
Unfolding her heart.
Life's sacred lover,
To seek within,
You heal me to know
You are the one.

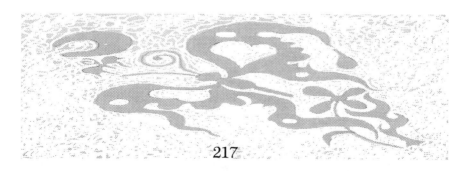

The Galactic Cherub

I wished upon a star,
And it fell.
Was kneeling on my wings,
And I couldn't tell.
No excuse,
Though heaven's not here,
 I just didn't know
 I'm supposed To be an angel.

The Planet of Sharing

Miraculous, this carved rock
Circling a suspended fire,
This granular of stars and sky
Leaves a breath that
I'm home.
The rain was too late;
Your food has died pretty.
The seed was scattered And in another belly.

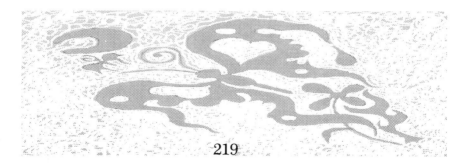

Bit Deeper

I was just thinking of you.
While you feel it,
Be it,
Live it.
Who are you?
What preciousness have I unearthed?
A rare love,
Or a trust you deserve?

The Mirrored Hemisphere

I thought I had seen this,
Or dreamt as a dream.
Been here before,
Now realities weaned.
Subconscious is sharply dwelling,
Reflecting in me:
I am the mystical uniqueness
Of a miraculous entity.

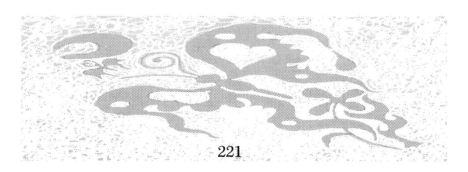

The Earthbound Smile

A powerful vibe of tingling warmth
Grows strength to this heart.
Plants twist to chase the fireball
Until the evening star.
Venus, she walks this planet,
She chose us and exchanged her wings.
She doesn't need to fly
When you hear my love sing.

_In_

Writing on this paper mirror,
Vulnerability is free to embrace.
You've burnt an angel in my brain
With your pretty face.
Only you can melt me,
Only you get that close;
Truly your love's my elixir,
Breathing the sweetest dose.

dean pusell 2013 (c)

Journeying Me Free

A fault no love divided,
Come back to me in you.
I dream of you awake,
I'm lying here true.
The sun's sweetest yellow light
Illuminated the eyes of the vessel's soul;
Your spirit's only alive
When you don't need to be told.

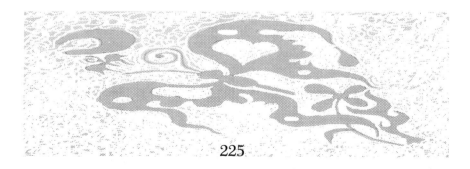

The Fruitful Nurture

I am hunger,
awaiting the most delicate seedling.
I am fear,
Hoping its life will feed me.
A fired sky warms us patiently;
I slurped a raindrop.
My appreciation will feast
Till this mortal heart does stop.

Courage like a Butterfly

The undefinable creator
Was cladding flesh on the lights.
A comprehension of the finite
Is all you need to enjoy tonight.
I've spilt my heart in trust;
It was caught by the prettiest soul.
She poured it all back so fresh,
Her smiles took away the cold.

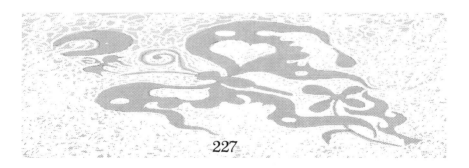

Delve the Hint

Waste not, being of presumption,
 Just pursue your sacred essence,
Nestle in the clarity,
For now is your present.
This realm is a blink—
Egotistically I've smashed the rules,
But my lights undercurrent pulse
Now stops the synchronisation to fools.

Tune to Absorb

Seek value in the journey
Over the success of destination.
I am meant to be where I'm at,
In compassion's preservation.
Such temporary visitors
On this planet of matter.
Treasure beyond the five sensors,
Or the three-dimensional world will scatter.

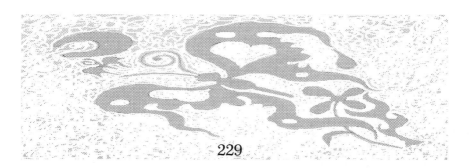

Earthing for All

The barren enchanter's plea
Illustrates the frequency:
A depth so shallow
There's only self-occupancy.
So use that eyed mind,
Open that sacred heart.
If it's only I's path,
Query the end to parts.

The Man made Men

This terminal physical vessel
Flows an entropy from the moon.
Gravitate and magnetise love,
For your flowing light will leave soon.
Leave the leaves shining,
Let the trees breathe.
The Godless status structures
Take up space for seed.

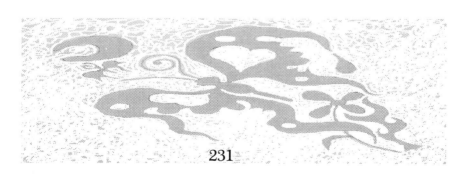

A Sibling to Wisdom

Devoted to sacrifice,
Discovered I'm a living chore,
Faced I'm a slave
To my limited core.
A mastery, block by block,
I'll bridge that complexity of lies,
Told them too long to myself,
But now I've got three eyes.

A Being of Gratitude's Attitude

Endure the short, bitter daze;
Change will cleanse it all,
Rich seasons of freshness.
You too can rejuvenate from small.
Befriend their mirrored hurt;
Their hidden lesson isn't clear.
The sign of centred timing
Will explain their rooted fear.

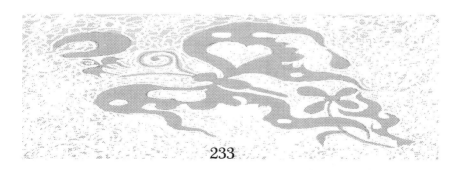

Vision of a Fertile Idea

The way you see things
Is the way you'll be:
A worn path to haven,
My grown guise of identity.
An uncharted churning
In a tender tendency,
This precious presence
Unmasks love sacredly.

Past the Past

I've languished in a vacuum of thoughts,
From cradle to here.
I've uttered limited logic;
I belong how?
Smack that sting;
Am I a piece of God's mind?
Infinite patience shall bring,
Only now matters this time.

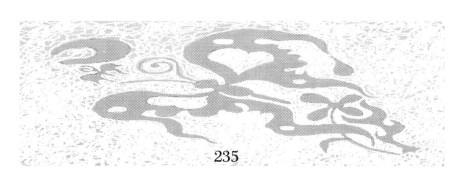

Programmed Patient

Ringlets flowing into each other,
The skies throwing droplets again,
Pond lilies ripple
As lavender lotuses pretend.
Why won't you be open today?
 I want to see your beauty.
What cloud?
Whose duty?

Trust You

As a king parrot screams past,
I thought to find the right questions,
And you will live the right answer
Without contemplation.
I see God in smiles;
It blooms my heart
Like a whip-bird smack,
Waking from dark.

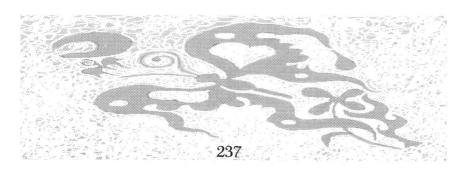

The Sleepy I

Where does this fit?
 It's only me,
Ambiguously fresh
To be a craving seed,
Never aware of my centre
Till the valid question begins.
So I tore this shell open
And let me burst forth from within.

Breathe

I meditated in front of a mushroom;
The sun was sliding down a tree.
Beauty smashed me like sunlight,
Well beyond illusion's sensory.
I never ate the mushroom;
I did see the star white Venus
Encrusted in the brightest blue,
Wrapped in a celestial womb.

Embodiment

Is awareness appreciating intricacy?
I give beyond my stash;
In this meat there's a secret,
An essence riddled with truth.
You can come to my light;
I have two candles left,
Love the way they paint your face
And sway at every breath.

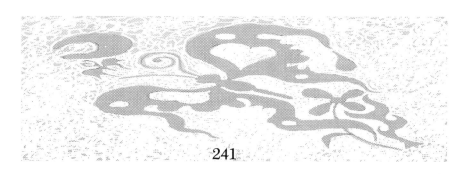

A Hole in Empty

I crouch down wishing for sun,
Dreaming of warmth.
But you left,
And I didn't know me, torn.
That's not dry skin—
You're a serpent of take.
Shed on someone else,
I'm too fresh awake.

Realming Delta

Inhale that reflection,
Don't let them live in their heads,
Quench that heart,
Pull back the dreads.
Know we've never met,
I'm no one else in me.
Travel in love's truth,
Contentment is smiling free.

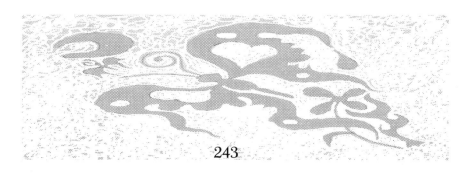

Out

I saw it:
They are connected to the heart.
Your squint hides nothing—
Why would a waterfall block its beauty?
Let feelings flow for something.
I was here,
But am I awake?
Let the seeking begin, with in, within.

Climbing Nurture

Who peaks this mountain,
Or is your view silence?
What makes you high
With feelings of timelessness?
I shed my labels;
The scars were stories.
I'm different now,
Soaking in deeper glories.

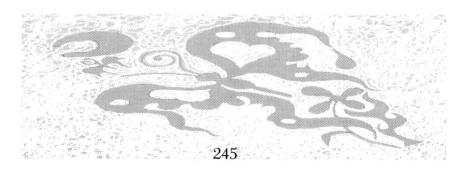

Don't Beat Awake

Why do you destroy the healer
And treat them weak and lost?
You're pained in ignorance;
I forgave your cost.
Dream a little deeper,
Deeper than skin,
Watch the signs flirt
  Lighting shadows with a grin.

Thread

The sounds of water,
A raindrop or an ocean crash.
You tickled me
As I pulled web from your body.
I'd never cocoon your being;
Freedom is essence.
We mirror smiles
That open the presence.

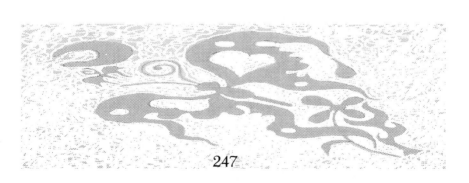

The Dying Narcissist Dims

In a powerful existence,
I am like a distant jellyfish,
Transparently floating emotions,
Feeling so selfish.
Of course there's a God,
Or isn't this the prettiest mistake?
So thrive in your opportunity,
To share more than you take.

Pollination

The site of innocence,
Dreamt sight,
I see the dance in freedom
As the choice flows alight.
Two hearts and a star
Squint away from machines.
Let be as it is?
Or live what you believe.

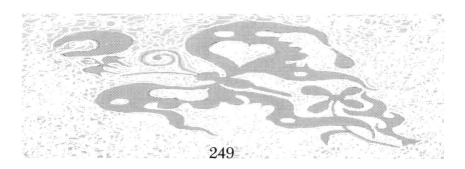

Circled Love

Happy tears, kaleidoscope flames—
This moment's unique.
You're only thieving a placebo,
Trying to live it again.
This twilight I sleep alone,
Drifting our dreamy symbols,
Rest as we balance home,
 In a planet's caress of people.

Left Here

So that's your clock,
And who's your time?
Somewhere in a way
To yourself, you've lied.
So I've tangled vanity,
Slowly dreaded the chase.
Now if I am of well-being?
Love is the humble space.

Conformed to Reptilian

Quiver at slightness,
It's blurred the vision,
The sensitive reflection
Went back past.
Rippling clarity
Mused the message awake.
Cut free now, puppet,
Controlled by a snake.

Peel to Empathy

I did seek around the roar
In a midnight sky splash.
That's not the moon, it's a bulb,
We can tell.
Can't fake perfection,
Though the unfathomable design's cursed.
Too many lost egos on a rock,
So stroke kindness in its worst.

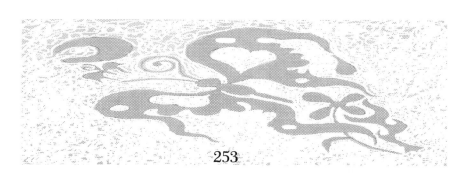

Incite Insight

I dodge their dark vibe
Like a poisonous vapour;
This one can centre
In the stable heart of trust.
Thieve nothing from me,
For I will share.
Life does trip to bliss;
Believing is not a dare.

Knew You from Nest

You little breather,
All soft and smiley,
You chase off fear
Faster than regrets.
Beside me like air,
Your loyalty brings colour.
You paint me safe,
Where the serpents bother.

Sheltering Sacred

You're new to this wake,
Yet no one died.
Your mind's opening,
A bloom in a purposeful surprise.
So what do you see from the sea?
I'm vertical horizon,
She's close at a distance
And securely free from prising.

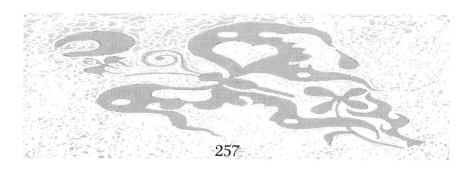

Dream Chasing Materialised

The cracking mirror of feelings—
I tasted your salty tears.
She surrendered to her grounding,
And I listened to her fears.
No suffering in loyalty
For the chosen one,
In her, him,
Beneath the winter's sun.

The Nest, Earth

At the dusk of a heart's roost,
I nestle in the trust of meditation;
This sanctuary of peace
Flows the answer in reflection.
Dreams are everything,
Or is reality more?
But love, love is my muse,
From the stars to the earthy floor.

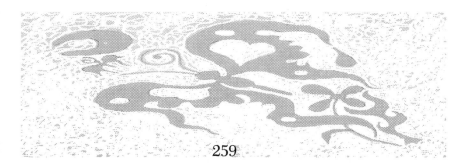

Flux

I see time shadowing faster,
So I blow on the embers
Like it's your pulse of love,
The kindest flame.
So close, you're in my body,
This mind, heart, and smile.
I'll carry you so deeply,
In eternity's mile.

Eagles Circle an Angel

I watched wings for you,
So you're to dream again,
You, the prey in their eyes,
Drift vulnerably asleep.
You didn't know they swooped you
With the sun on your pretty face.
Love made my fear blind
As I sheltered your sacred space.

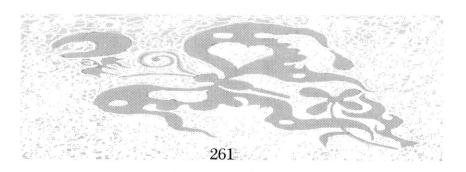

I Volunteer Yours

If this is mine,
Then here is yours,
'Cause this rhythm that loves you
Is my coronary of trust.
The rainbow will vapour,
But our love can stay.
It all started as a spark
But now flames our way.

<u>Shaking Shadows</u>

Maybe I'm nothing in the eye of this mind?
Maybe I'm something in the throb of this heart?
But know twice this breathing experience:
We are pure choice in this part.
Dissect and decipher all gathered truths,
Closer to your deepest meaning.
Smile at a miscalculated love,
Allude to all your eyes of assuming.

The Surging Emulation

In this humble heart of thunder,
My spirit's a spark in the forest,
Nourishing the receptors of beauty,
Forgiving all answers.
Within the shy dreamer plunged,
Swimming through whispers and uncertainties,
To be in one I peeled fear,
Surrendering to the princess my vulnerability.

Motion

No chemical enhancement assisted this vision,
But the true illusion was the sharp need to wander
Awake in my dreams,
Bringing me closer and deeper, inside, out.
So I, in eye, journey this little being,
Exposing devolved imperfections,
But the speculum of truth
Embraced no separation in any direction.

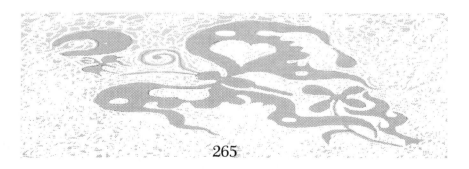

Bee Here 28 Days

You're in the direction of the winter sun,
With sticky wings and sweet knees,
A nectar seeping such love
Only she can be the one.
Why cares to fly
When this garden's the gift?
Gather the fruit of trust,
For it will nurture swift.

Our Bedazzling Phosphoresce

The fireball rises to fade stars,
Its light flaming the wet forest.
Glistening droplets reflect sky blue
In the echoes of winged chants.
Fresh freedom is a truth:
Believe and it will awaken.
Do your best, sweet being,
Alive is giving before you're taken.

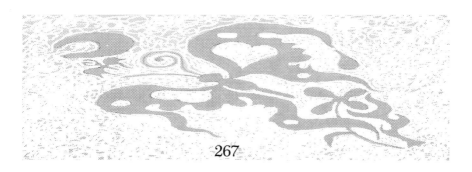

The Psyche Theatre Heeds a Haven

These deep breathing thoughts
Flood imagery of splendour.
Are you love?
Welcome, I dream of you.
What follows the last sight
Beyond the blind boundaries?
The breeze feels like angels
Taking me home within their journeys.

Her Inner Star Tune

Her angelic spirit smiles,
Shining eyes uniquely earth truth,
Rooted in a cherished heart,
The faith of a lioness.
Her dreamy aura resonates peace,
Bewilderment's ore blooms like lotus,
Together we're freedom,
Serenely celestial vibes entwine us.

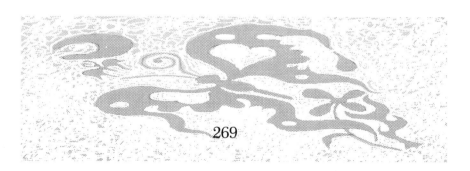

269

The Occupant Beneath

A silver root of light anchors my soul.
Am I the host to a ghost?
I've learnt you in pain,
I've loved you in love.
So my befriended essence,
Translate our bind?
Vitality's breath in the vehicle,
So conscious in matter sublime.

Eyes of Spirit

As a being of this fresh seasonal realm,
Dwelling on God's earthy craft,
Her voice of soft divine music,
Kept another secret for me.
I love the peace in trust,
The sync pulse of no uncertainty,
Hearts floating around the sun,
Nurturing our mirrored lights consciously.

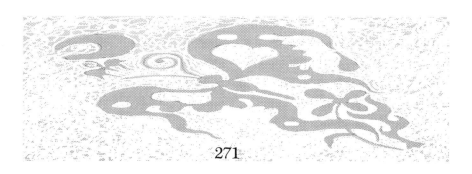

The Sacred Connectedness of Love

My consciousness has evolved enough
To comprehend this existence is equivalent
To a grasp of a dream, mentally unfathomable.
The only potency is the truth of this moment,
 In which we ripple back to the mercy of a superior
 Creator.

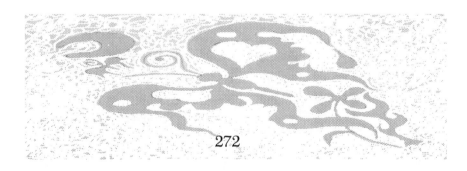

www.deanpusell.com